D1292513

ANCIENT WARRIORS

SPARTANS

KENNY ABDO

Fly!
An Imprint of Abdo Zoom
abdobooks.com

abdobooks.com

Published by Abdo Zoom, a division of ABDO, P.O. Box 398166, Minneapolis, Minnesota 55439. Copyright © 2021 by Abdo Consulting Group, Inc. International copyrights reserved in all countries. No part of this book may be reproduced in any form without written permission from the publisher. Fly!™ is a trademark and logo of Abdo Zoom.

Printed in the United States of America, North Mankato, Minnesota.
102020
012021

 THIS BOOK CONTAINS
RECYCLED MATERIALS

Photo Credits: Alamy, Everett Collection, Granger Collection, iStock, North Wind Picture Archives, Shutterstock
Production Contributors: Kenny Abdo, Jennie Forsberg, Grace Hansen
Design Contributors: Dorothy Toth, Neil Klinepier, Laura Graphenteen

Library of Congress Control Number: 2019956191

Publisher's Cataloging-in-Publication Data

Names: Abdo, Kenny, author.
Title: Spartans / by Kenny Abdo
Description: Minneapolis, Minnesota : Abdo Zoom, 2021 | Series: Ancient warriors | Includes online resources and index.
Identifiers: ISBN 9781098221263 (lib. bdg.) | ISBN 9781098222246 (ebook) | ISBN 9781098222734 (Read-to-Me ebook)
Subjects: LCSH: Greece--Sparta (Extinct city)--Juvenile literature. | Armed Forces--Juvenile literature. | Civilization--Juvenile literature. | Military art and science--Juvenile literature. | Soldiers--Juvenile literature.
Classification: DDC 938.9--dc23

TABLE OF CONTENTS

SPARTANS

Highly trained and utterly brutal, the Spartans stopped at nothing to protect their home.

While others studied art, history, and philosophy, the Spartans lived and breathed war.

THE WARRIORS

Sparta was a powerful **city-state** in Ancient Greece. The city-state rose to such strength because it had a strong army to protect it.

Every male in Sparta was raised by their mothers until the age of 7. Then they went to Spartan school, called the **agōgē**.

11

The **agōgē** had a strict training program that prepared boys to become warriors. The main focuses were on **endurance** and **strategy**.

13

WARFARE & TACTICS

Spartan males became full-time soldiers at 20 years old. They stayed on **active duty** until they were 60.

4

Training and hard work made Spartans skilled fighters. To be even stronger, they would fight in **phalanx formation**.

Spartans carried a short sword called a xiphos. Their most important weapon was the shield. If they lost their shield in battle, they would suffer great shame.

The Battle of Thermopylae took place in 480 BCE. Just 7,000 Spartans clashed with more than 70,000 Persian soldiers. They were defeated, but not without a fight.

The end of Sparta began in 371 BCE, after being defeated by the Thebes army in the Battle of Leuctra. Along with its state, so fell the Spartan army.

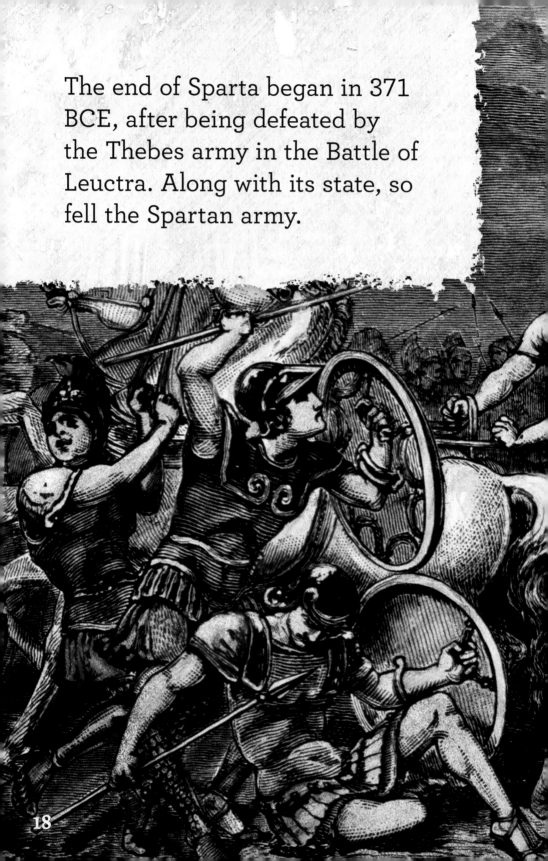

ARE YOU NOT ENTERTAINED?!

The Battle of Thermopylae was famously retold in the Frank Miller comic *300*. It was later **adapted** into the hit movie of same name.

Today, people can participate in Spartan style **marathons** around the world. This is a vast improvement from vicious, nonstop wars.

GLOSSARY

active duty – someone who is in the military full time.

adapt – to change for a particular use, like from a book to a movie.

agōgē – a mandatory education and training program that all male Spartans attended.

city-state – a city that becomes an independent state with its surrounding territory.

endurance – the ability to go on under pain and hardship.

marathon – a long-distance race that is usually 26 miles (42.2 km) long.

phalanx formation – when a large group of soldiers stand close to each other, with long spears and interlocking shields.

strategy – a plan or series of actions meant to perform a particular goal or effect.

ONLINE RESOURCES

Booklinks
NONFICTION NETWORK
FREE! ONLINE NONFICTION RESOURCES

To learn more about Spartans, please visit abdobooklinks.com or scan this QR code. These links are routinely monitored and updated to provide the most current information available.

INDEX